The Fir

The First Waldorf Teachers

*Twelve Biographical Vignettes
of Leaders of the First School*

Tomas Zdrazil

Waldorf
PUBLICATIONS

The First Waldorf Teachers:
Twelve Biographical Vignettes
of Leaders of the First School
by
Tomas Zdrazil

published by

Waldorf Publications
351 Fairview Avenue, Unit 625
Hudson, NY 12534

© 2019 Waldorf Publications

ISBN: 978-1-943582-40-2

Contents

Introduction 1

Emil Molt 7

E. A. Karl Stockmeyer . . . 13

Herbert Hahn 19

Leonie von Mirbach 25

Caroline von Heydebrand . . . 31

Eugen Kolisko 37

Friedrich Oehlschlegel . . . 43

Walter Johannes Stein . . . 49

Alexander Strakosch 55

Karl Schubert 61

Elisabeth and Paul Baumann
Marriage of the Arts in the Waldorf School   67

Elisabeth Grunelius 73

Introduction

On April 23, 1919, Rudolf Steiner was asked by the Stuttgart entrepreneur Emil Molt to take on the pedagogical leadership of the school he planned to found, including the task of finding the teachers. Rudolf Steiner had devoted decades to establishing an anthroposophical view of the world. He thought Molt's initiative was highly important and looked upon the endeavor as a testcase for "the viability of the anthroposophical worldview."

Up to the end of World War I, anthroposophy was viewed by the public at large as little more than theory. Now came the moment when it should prove itself in pedagogical practice, for all to see. Steiner emphasized: "Anthroposophy is no mere theory; we should strive to apply it in practical life. At this point in time, what can be gained through anthroposophical understanding has to be turned into reality in the classroom."

Now it became a question of who could fit the bill. Of all those who had found a connection to anthroposophy by this time, who would be up to the task? Much was at stake. There was considerable risk that the venture would fail. To whom should Dr. Steiner turn to now, to start this endeavor?

Thus it came about be that he invited two dozen people to take part in a preparatory course, which took place in Stuttgart right before the school was to be inaugurated. A large majority of the participants was actively involved in a campaign for social renewal. Most of them were highly educated and well versed in the anthroposophical world picture which Steiner had been building up. Many were long-term members of the anthroposophical Society; indeed, five of them were even branch leaders. In considering the ones who had a traditional teacher training, Steiner was especially careful. "In my task of composing the faculty of teachers for the Waldorf school, I do not consider academic qualifications an obstacle *per se*. However, I will say that I am more vigilant when people have academic certificates for teaching, especially when it comes to determining whether a person has the necessary human qualities to be a teacher. When people have academic teacher certificates, it is always good to be extra cautious …."

Of the eight teachers with traditional teacher qualifications, interestingly enough, he selected only four to join the Waldorf faculty, and of those four people, two stepped back after only a short time. Most of the faculty members were very young, their average age being no more than 34. However, in that they had no experience in the classroom, they were largely unencumbered by tradition, routine, procedure, etc. Among them we find a variety of professions including artists, clergy, a doctor, and an engineer.

Within the anthroposophical movement, Waldorf teachers were highly regarded. In the words of Rudolf Grosse, a pupil in the Stuttgart school and later a leader in the anthroposophical world, "To be a Waldorf teacher was a unique accolade among anthroposophists, an honor given to those who were spiritual pioneers, and there was no greater distinction than being asked by Rudolf Steiner to join the faculty of teachers at the Waldorf school." Steiner wanted these men and women to feel they were culture bearers, acolytes in an act of cultural renewal to which they would dedicate themselves completely. "We will only be able to reach our goal, when each individual gives his/her all. Right from the start, every single individual must be fully committed.... Every individual is to be fully responsible."

Rudolf Steiner never worked as intensively in his life with a group of people as he did with the first circle of Waldorf teachers, giving himself fully to the extensive work in the preparatory course of two weeks. He placed the success of this school in their hands, and stressed the immeasurable importance of their task. "This Waldorf school must succeed!" At the closure of the course on September 6, 1919, he added a personal remark. "For me personally, this Waldorf school will be a veritable child of care. Again and again I shall have to come back to this Waldorf school with anxious, caring thoughts."

With the twelve short portraits* presented here on the occasion of the beginning of the second century of the Waldorf schools movement, my aim is to give readers a chance both to form a concrete, living picture of the views which stood at the birth of the school, and to become acquainted with a few of the most prominent personalities of the first generation of Waldorf teachers.

---

* These sketches first appeared in the magazine *Erziehungskunst*, starting in July/August 2018 and ending in September 2019. For readers wishing to gain a more thorough understanding of the Waldorf School during the period of time it was led by Rudolf Steiner himself, see Tomas Zdazil, *Freie Waldorfschule in Stuttgart 1919-1925. Rudolf Steiner - das Kollegium - die Pädagogik* (Stuttgart: edition waldorf, 2019).

Emil Molt

Emil Molt

Rudolf Steiner had given indications since 1906 on how spiritual science could provide insights for education, but it was not until 1919 that the Stuttgart entrepreneur Emil Molt helped to make Rudolf Steiner's pedagogical insights a reality. "He was small and stocky, and his portly figure, with a large, bald head and fine features, suggested a man of strong will. He had small, blue eyes which were very lively and intelligent, and he looked at you with a penetrating gaze. His mouth was large, his lips thin, and his chin was firmly set, all of which made his face decidedly attractive." (Rudolf Grosse)

Molt placed his life completely at the service of his company, the Waldorf Astoria cigarette factory, and he was singularly devoted to his workers and their families, including his office staff. They called him "father Molt", and they felt seen and appreciated by him. In the Waldorf Astoria company, workers did not go on strike as a way to negotiate; Molt founded recuperation homes for them and made sure their children had fresh milk to drink. He instituted a company bulletin called *Waldorf News* ("Waldorf Nachrichten") so that his factory had an internal organ to facilitate communication and education.

One of Molt's most important deeds was to organize adult education courses for his workers. He was bursting at the seams with a will to accomplish things and work for social change. He weighed various options with his wife, Berta, to use the company's profits to benefit the workers: founding a retirement home, launching a home for the children, or starting a school. The last option won out.

On April 23, 1919, the Molts unfolded the idea to Rudolf Steiner, whom the Molts had known as their teacher for quite some time and Emil Molt asked him to take on the pedagogical leadership of the school. His request marked the beginning of a long period of intense collaboration as the two men worked to build up the school. Together with a small group of people, Emil Molt and Rudolf Steiner engaged in many strategic planning sessions as well as excruciatingly tough meetings in times of crisis; they spent countless hours driving back and forth between Dornach and Stuttgart; they experienced intense closeness as well as painful separations.

Something which linked Steiner and Molt closely together was their ability to see the interconnectedness of deep spiritual insight and practical work. Molt came to see how correct Steiner's admonition was that anthroposophy would be able to reach its mission in civilization only when it could also find expression in architectural forms, and he made it his business to work hard for that ideal by involving himself in various architectural endeavors, lending his expertise to fundraising for buildings in Malsch, Dornach, and Stuttgart. He found and purchased a property in a hilly district of Stuttgart which could house the Waldorf school, and he shouldered the bulk of the cost of the first barracks which were built on the premises, as well as the large school building which came soon thereafter.

A high point in Molt's biography was the opening festival of the school, held on September 7, 1919. He looked upon the thriving Waldorf school as the biggest gift of his life, and he remained intensely involved with all the early phases of its development. His wife Berta, "the soul of his life," served on the faculty as a handwork teacher. His son Walter caused many a stir with his pranks as a student in this new school, not least of which was his avid efforts to distribute cigarettes among his fellow students. His misbehavior caused a number of situations which were embarrassing for Emil in his role as father not only of his mischievous son but of the school.

Molt led an intensely religious life. Not only did he make it his business to maintain friendly ties with both Catholics and Protestants in Stuttgart, but, next to providing denominational instruction, he also was highly committed to instituting free religious lessons within the school, including Sunday services. He was also actively involved in the later founding of the Christian Community. After Hitler had come to power, Molt played an exemplary and farsighted role in making sure the school took an uncompromising stance against the Nazi leadership. Until his death in 1936, he was able to shield the school from various attempts on the part of the regime to gain a say in the school's governance and curriculum.

E.A. Karl Stockmeyer

E.A. Karl Stockmeyer

Next to Emil Molt, the founder of the Waldorf School, and Rudolf Steiner, the school's leader, there was a third person who filled a highly important role: that of administrator. It was E. A. Karl Stockmeyer who took on that task. He was 33 years old at the time, and was trained as a natural scientist. Among anthroposophists, he was the one teacher who, after World War I, was working in the public domain dealing with matters of educational policy.

From the end of the war in 1918, Stockmeyer had been working to develop original educational ideas based on Rudolf Steiner's *Philosophy of Freedom* and later impulses Steiner had given, ideas that could be implemented to rebuild the German educational system. Stockmeyer published several papers on the subject.

In January 1919, Emil Molt asked Stockmeyer to help in the founding of an independent school in Stuttgart. Stockmeyer first imagined he would be a consultant in the planning process of the school, but things took a different turn when Steiner accepted the position of school leader. At his request, Stockmeyer changed his plans at the end of April 1919 and asked for a leave of absence from his state school in order to join the faculty of the Stuttgart school.

In designing a curriculum, it was quite a struggle for him to work with Steiner's ideas, since it meant letting go of conventions and drawing up something original and uninfluenced by state curricula. It was also hard for him to imagine anything other than a classical state school schedule. But he adjusted. He also took on the task of finding the future group of colleagues, and in July he embarked on a "voyage of discovery" to find the first circle of Waldorf teachers. Rudolf Steiner jokingly said he should go "collect the *stars*."

In August 1919, Stockmeyer and his family relocated to Stuttgart and moved into an apartment in the new school building. He took on organizing the preparatory course for the new cohort of teachers and all subsequent faculty courses; getting the building ready as well as furniture and school supplies, making the schedule, leading the faculty meetings, communicating with the school officials, and carrying the entire administration of the school.

In his teaching tasks, Stockmeyer focused on the natural sciences of the upper grades. Many subjects in the areas of "practical arts and technology," such as surveying, were introduced into the curriculum by him. He took care of communication between Steiner and the faculty, always maintaining an extraordinarily sovereign position towards him: "His very posture showed this during faculty meetings, where he would be sitting with his hand supporting his chin, weighing every word and pondering it."

Rudolf Steiner was eager for Stockmeyer to earn a PhD, just like Herbert Hahn. But, with all he had to do, this was out of the question. Stockmeyer put all his scientific interests and questions on the back burner for the sake of administering the school, putting his whole life at the disposal of the practical and administrative side of founding the school. We owe it to him that the organizational miracle of the school's founding succeeded and that ties to the local authorities were consistently good.

In addition, the administering of the fledgling Waldorf School Association (the organization responsible for financing the school) rested largely on Stockmeyer's shoulders. During the economic crisis years of 1922/23, he several hundred letters seeking help from sponsors, inside and outside of Germany. Who knows if the [school] would have survived if he hadn't done all that work?

[Sto]ckmeyer's phlegmatic temperament stood him [in goo]d stead, for it carried him through this stressful [adm]inistrative work. He also had an innate sense for sculpture and architecture, qualities that helped shape the social edifice of the whole undertaking.

Stockmeyer remained faithful to the school until it was forced to close in 1938, at which time he steadfastly carried through the administrative aspect of the closure procedures. Then he had to write an application letter for a teacher's position. "The work in the Waldorf School, which was led until 1925 by Rudolf Steiner, the most eminent German philosopher, spiritual researcher, and a trailblazing educator, has given me unbelievably strong and fruitful impulses and experiences I couldn't have gained in any other way, all of which I feel obliged to make fruitful for public education for the remainder of my life," he wrote. This was an honest and singularly courageous letter to write in 1940. A political assessment, drawn up around the same time by the NSDAP [National Socialist Party], stated: "Stockmeyer was a fanatical anthroposophist. He played a dominant part in the anthroposophical leadership of the Waldorf School, was a member of the Waldorf School Council, and headed the 100 Waldorf Ortsgruppen [local school groups throughout Germany to fund the Waldorf schools]. He took a sharp stance against National Socialism, even after the party came to power. He is chiefly responsible for the negative position taken by the Waldorf School faculty. Both philosophically and politically, he is to be rejected, and would be unsuitable as a teacher." Nevertheless, he managed to secure a teacher's position in Königsfeld, but his entire anthroposophical library was seized by the Gestapo. After

1945, he helped found the first Waldorf school in Freiburg. He was also responsible for the first systematic outline of the Waldorf elementary school curriculum. In retirement he continued to work on questions of epistemology and Waldorf pedagogy until his death in 1963.

"His mind was shaped by exact philosophical schooling, and as a thinker he stood on his own feet."
(Herbert Hahn)

Herbert Hahn

Herbert Hahn

In the spring of 1919, Emil Molt managed to attract Herbert Hahn to coordinate and teach education courses that Molt had set up for his workers in the Waldorf Astoria cigarette factory. Hahn, 28 at the time, was working as a translator. He had grown up in Pernau, Estonia, surrounded by the light-filled, expansive Baltic landscape, where he moved easily in a multilingual environment. Hahn was endowed with great inner versatility, was receptive to an infinite variety of sense impressions, and was greatly interested in all the nuances of interpersonal relationships. These qualities he combined with an ability to catch the fullness of his experiences in highly pictorial and nuanced language.

When he came to Stuttgart in 1919, Hahn was amply prepared, having studied in Dorpat, Heidelberg, Paris, and Berlin. With additional diplomas from Pernau and Moscow, he seemed destined for a career in academia. However, when Rudolf Steiner met him back in 1909, he advised him otherwise, pointing him towards a future of teaching languages in a new way. He was able to start work on this in the continuing education courses in an adult education school Molt was setting up for the workers. This school, and the motivation behind it, helped prepare the birth of the Waldorf School. Its aim was to teach in a way that went beyond specialization, helping workers engaged within the narrow confines of an industrial environment expand their horizons and preserve their humanity. What the workers experienced there intensified their wish for a school that would cultivate the same spirit in their children.

Having gained the trust of the workers, Hahn was tasked with leading preparatory parent evenings which paved the way for the founding of the school. When the Waldorf School started, he first taught foreign languages, but his tasks soon multiplied. He continued to work in the education courses for the workers, was much in demand as an anthroposophical lecturer, and wrote a dissertation for his PhD at the University of Greifswalt. In his third year at the school he became class teacher of the third grade and was chosen to be part of the newly instituted Leadership Council of the school. He remained at the Stuttgart school until 1931.*

As early as September 1919, Hahn was asked to build up the school's religion lessons, with the consequence that he became the first teacher to hold Sunday services connected with the lessons. What qualified him to conduct these services for the children was his unique combination of a profound inwardness and a highly artistic and imaginative way of describing nature. Looking back, a former student said of Hahn: "He combined a remarkably fine and cultured way of expressing himself with a warmth of heart which was a balm for everyone, a combination which none of the other teachers possessed. As a result, we instinctively felt we could trust him, even though he always retained a respectful distance from the students." (Grosse, 1998, p. 88)

A central motive of Hahn's life was to contribute to a better understanding of the different nations, based on a comprehensive, deep spiritual understanding of languages. This lifelong preoccupation found its culmination in his major work *Vom Genius Europas*.

Herbert Hahn had a very special gift in the social realm.

---

* Herbert Hahn then moved to Holland, where he lived from 1931 until after the war. Thereupon he returned to the "mother-school" and worked there until 1961

He was able to work together with the most diverse groups of people and build bridges between opposing camps to such an extent that he became accepted by more or less all of his colleagues. We are also in his debt for his many highly differentiated and empathetic characterizations of all the teachers who worked in the first Waldorf school. He lived to a ripe old age and remained a living conscience of the school movement until his death in 1970.

Leonie von Mirbach

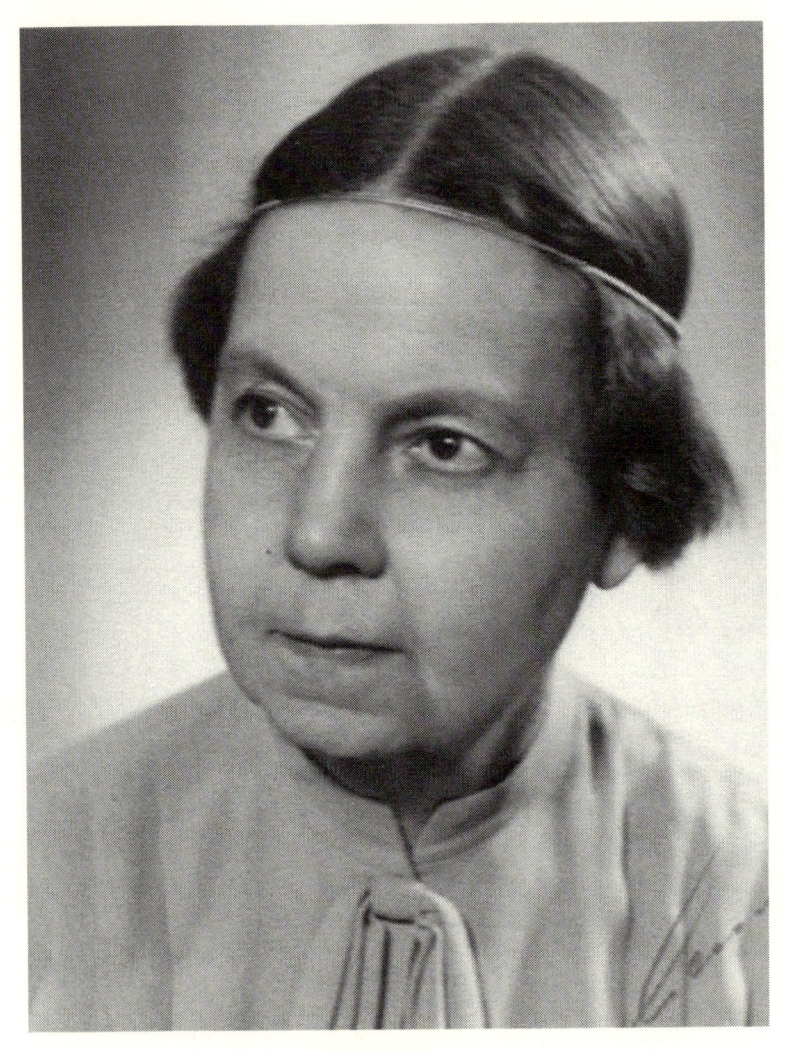

Leonie von Mirbach

Rudolf Steiner waited until the end of the preparatory teacher training course before announcing who would take which class or subject. Even though 24 participants attended the course, only 12 of them were employed during the first year. It seems that Steiner had not involved anybody from this first—apart from Herbert Hahn and Karl Stockmeyer—in the selection of the primary positions of class teachers, even though this was an existential question for those involved. Faced with the reality of paying salaries for twelve teachers, even Emil Molt was surprised and somewhat taken aback when he realized how quickly the sum he had initially put aside would be used up.

Young as she was, Leonie von Mirbach was given the historic appointment as the first grade teacher in the first Waldorf school. Her early childhood destiny had been marked by drama. Ernst, her father, came from an honorable old aristocratic family in the Rhineland, her mother Lida from a poor Lithuanian family. Such a marriage was highly unusual in those days. For that reason they traveled to Egypt, where he set up shop as a businessman. It was there that Leonie and her three sisters were born.

However, her father lost his entire fortune and died of typhoid fever when Leonie was two years old. After that, the family moved to Lithuania, where they lived in the poorest circumstances for eight years. In 1901, Leonie was adopted by her grandmother and Aunt von Mirbach. They lived in Tübingen, where she received an excellent education and passed her high school exam, but she was very sickly as a child. The family became involved with anthroposophy during the time they lived in Tübingen.

Both of von Mirbachs's two older sisters felt connected to anthroposophy as well. At the time that the call came to join the Waldorf school, Leonie was studying in Halle, majoring in an unusual combination of subjects: biology and philosophy. She had been involved in the effort to work with the movement for social threefolding, after which she applied for a position in the Waldorf school which was about to be founded.

In hiring Leonie von Mirbach, Steiner had to accept a certain complication, which was that she needed to remain in Halle until the end of October of that year in order to complete her final exams. Walter Johannes Stein substituted for her at the beginning of the year, which means he was the first Waldorf teacher to introduce the lesson of "straight line and curve". Also it was he who, after bringing the straight letter I and the curved C on day one, came with the idea to introduce the letter H the next day, so that "ich"—the German word for "I"—became the first word the children learned. Von Mirbach arrived after this lesson had taken place, and took over her first-graders, 34 in all.

The number of children in her class grew, so that by end of the first year of school there were 41, a number which reached 53 by the beginning of the second school year. During the discussions in the faculty meeting, Rudolf Steiner greatly praised Leonie's work, and was equally complementary about her collection of poems and stories, which he called "proof of the spirit which reigns in the Waldorf school". Later these became the basis for the reader *Der Sonne Licht*, later translated into English as *The Sun With Loving Light*.

Von Mirbach's gift for the word comes to expression both in this collection and in the verses she wrote for the reports of her first-graders. She was the first class teacher to give all the children of her class this gift of report verses written especially for them. A few examples follow:

Lernen im Lichte zu schauen die Schönheit.
[Learn to see beauty in light].

Fleißiges Lernen gibt dir für's Leben Freude und Kraft.
[Learning with all your might gives joy and strength for your whole life.]

Vertraue Dich frei der führenden Hand. Wage die Wege,
Die sie Dir weist.
[Freely trust the hand that guides you.
Venture out to follow where it leads you.]

Suche mit Ernst des Könnens Kraft.
[Earnestly seek the strength of achievement.]

After two years her health deteriorated. She was first assisted by Helene Grunelius in second grade, but still her health declined to the point that she had to hand over her class to Herbert Hahn. Even though she never worked as a class teacher in Stuttgart again, she kept in touch with Waldorf schools and lived to the ripe old age of 83.

Caroline von Heydebrand

Caroline von Heydebrand

In June 1919, Caroline von Heydebrand, like Leonie von Mirbach, applied for a position at the Waldorf School. She was 32 years old at the time, and was about to get her PhD at the University of Greifswald. Von Heydebrand, who came from an aristocratic family in Silesia, was broadly educated; she was well-versed in the classics, spoke several foreign languages, and was thoroughly steeped in anthroposophy.

Rudolf Steiner entrusted the fifth grade to her, which with forty-seven students was the biggest class in the school. She was delicately built and small of stature. Some of her students were as tall as she was! Her voice was so thin and high-pitched that it was hard for her at the beginning to establish herself in her teacher role. Her class consisted of a mixture of children from all kinds of different types of school and social background. Children of the workers at the Waldorf Astoria factory sat next to Felix Goll, the adopted son of the rich factory owner and founder of the school Emil Molt, something which was unheard of at the time. At the beginning of the school year there was no school furniture so the students sat on chairs left over from the days when the building had housed a restaurant, skidding around on the polished floors. One can hardly imagine a more challenging situation for a young, beginning teacher who began without teacher training or classroom experience.

But von Heydebrand met the challenge with characteristic intensity, tenacity, and artistry. She introduced the children to Greek culture, telling them stories from mythology and using sculptures for illustrations. She told them about the Greek gods and heroes, and had them draw Greek motives to go with the stories. She soon succeeded in winning the children's hearts, and they called her "Fräulein Doktor" [Miss Dr.].

Right after the war, there were enormous differences in skill levels among the students, both in German language and in mathematics, which presented her with considerable challenges. However, she had a thorough command of the material, both because she was highly educated and because she prepared assiduously; in short order she made great strides, especially because she was able to penetrate everything with great imagination.

She paired meticulous lesson planning with sensitive child observations. In addition, she began early on to write pedagogical publications containing highly detailed reflections based on her classroom experience. Steiner was able to observe her classes and often singled her out for praise in his lectures on the new art of education, holding her up as an example of how to integrate anthroposophical insights. She often accompanied him on his lecture tours to England, which felt like a second home to her.

In this way von Heydebrand became a master of the new art of education and devoted her whole life to it. She wrote a number of artistic texts to be used in the classroom, put together readers, edited the first magazine devoted to Waldorf pedagogy, wrote articles, gave lectures, and trained new teachers. Spurred on by Rudolf Steiner, she gained a thorough knowledge of the pedagogical renewal efforts prevalent in Germany at the time, drawing attention to their narrow focus on cognitive development, and observing how little such theories were able to contribute to a healthy and living practice in the classroom.

Three classes had the great pleasure of having her as

their class teacher. In 1935 she felt compelled to step back from teaching due to health reasons, political pressures, and tensions within the faculty. She died in the summer of 1938 after the Stuttgart school had been closed by the National Socialists, who had already banned her publications. She can truly be called one of the most eminent pioneers of Waldorf pedagogy, both because of her outstanding pedagogical contributions and her publications.

Eugen Kolisko

Eugen Kolisko

In December 1919, Friedrich Oehlschlegel, who was teaching sixth grade, unexpectedly departed for America, whereupon Hermann Heisler, a theologian from Tübingen, was asked to take his place. Heisler had been part of the preparatory course the previous summer, but had not been offered a teaching position at the time. Now he was hesitant to take the class, and declined. Molt therefore quickly sent the following telegram to Eugen Kolisko, who was 26 at the time. "*Oehlschlegel to America for Waldorf College. Please substitute straightaway. Room ready.*"

Kolisko had been teaching chemistry to physicians at the University of Vienna since 1917. He was a highly gifted, universally educated scientist, fully steeped in anthroposophy, and was first in line to be chosen as a teacher in an independent "Waldorf College", which was to be founded on anthroposophical principles. Early building plans drawn up for the Stuttgart school grounds included a building earmarked to house such a college.

Kolisko had studied medicine, not education, and up to that moment he had taught students only at the university level. He had never worked with children, and now he had to take over a pretty rambunctious sixth grade. He started with a biology block, the subject with which he was most familiar, followed by mathematics, German, and physics.

The first months were pretty much trial by fire for the young physician, who looked boyish and had a delicate constitution. His sober assessment was that "working with school children is much more challenging for a teacher than working at the college level, paradoxical as it may sound". His approach to the subject matter was both penetrating and alive, and he soon managed to win his students over and become a highly beloved teacher. Students liked to throng around him—they called him "Koli"—because he always had so much to offer. In the words of one of his students: "We couldn't get close enough, because we were so eager to absorb his words. His knowledge was suffused with his warm humanity".

In addition to his work in the classroom, Kolisko was most sought after in the endeavor to build up an independent "Hochschule" through a series of anthroposophical academic courses to renew and spiritualize science. Therefore he was in high demand to give courses, lectures, do research, and publish or edit books. Rudolf Steiner greatly valued his accomplishments as a researcher, as well as those of his wife Lili ("you feel in your heart that what he says is true, and he gives his all in pursuing this truth"). Steiner invited him to his major lecture cycles for young physicians, remedial teachers, and pastoral workers. Sadly, the planned Hochschule in Stuttgart did not materialize at that time.

Despit these obligations, Kolisko remained at the Stuttgart school. After an initial short stint as a class teacher, he taught a variety of subjects in the upper grades: history, English, and especially chemistry and biology. After 1921, he was freed up enough to take on the task of serving as school doctor, and in this capacity he very much used his newly acquired pedagogical insights. He was able inwardly to combine medical and pedagogical approaches in his work.

After the war, the health of many of his students was cause for concern. Kolisko helped in whatever way he could, not only as the school doctor but also in organizing and maintaining a soup kitchen, together with other teachers, to feed a number of undernourished children at no cost. Many of the medical-pedagogical indications Steiner gave were directly addressed to Kolisko.

After Steiner's death, a difficult time began for Kolisko as well as for his friend Walter Johannes Stein, and he suffered from various misunderstandings and conflicts. These circumstances necessitated his departure from Germany in 1934, and he spent the last five years of his life in England.

Friedrich Oehlschlegel

Friedrich Oehlschlegel

On the first day of school, 28 sixth graders were sitting in their tiny classroom under the roof of the newly adapted Waldorf School building, eagerly awaiting their teacher. "Suddenly, the door opens, everyone is watching. Friedrich Oehlschlegel enters. He's wearing a blue suit, a white shirt, and a green tie. He looks at us through gold-rimmed glasses, his eyes are blue and friendly." He greets his new class with a pronounced American accent, "Guten Morgen, liebe Kinder!" [Good morning, dear children].

With this first sentence, he immediately won the hearts of his children. Oehlschlegel had decided to focus on awakening an interest in the world, and pursued this in an unconventional way by doing geography almost exclusively during the first months. Despite his young age—he was only 28 years old—he had seen a lot of the world. One of his students, Fritz Koegel, who later became a Waldorf teacher, was very impressed. "The class became completely silent when he talked in geography class about his own journeys to Archangelsk or the Aral Sea."

Oehlschlegel, who had a German father and an American mother, grew up in the United States and worked there for a short time as a teacher. When World War I broke out, he decided to fight on the German side and traveled the Eastern route, crossing the Pacific to reach Europe. Wounded in battle, he was transported to a military hospital, where a nurse introduced him to anthroposophy. After the war he taught English at the University of Marburg. His originality and keen interest in anthroposophy motivated him to translate and discuss Steiner's *Kernpunkte der sozialen*

Frage [*Towards Social Renewal*] with the students in his seminars.

In this way he came in touch with the local branch of the Society for the Threefold Social Order in Marburg, where he learned about Emil Molt's plan to found a school in Stuttgart. He exchanged letters and met personally with Molt, who was charmed by Oehlschlegel and suggested he be invited to the opening course for the prospective Waldorf teachers. During the course, Herbert Hahn from the Baltic region, Walter Johannes Stein from Austria, and Oehlschlegel from America soon became fast friends; the three of them were close in age. During the discussions and workshops which took place alongside the lectures, we hear about Oehlschlegel giving a picture of the Mississippi River basin; at another occasion he did a presentation on introducing fractions, and when it came to speech exercises (*"Lieblich-Lippliche"*) he was made aware of the fact that his "L" was "still from the other side of the Atlantic."

Apart from class teaching and English, Oehlschlegel was given another assignment, together with his good friend Herbert Hahn: the highly responsible task to introduce a completely new subject, the free religion teaching for children of families without a specific religious denomination. It took a few months before the right form was established for this subject, including a service on Sundays. It was a sign of special confidence that Steiner entrusted Oehlschlegel with this task.

However, before he could hold the first services after the Christmas holidays of 1919/20, he decided to take on another assignment and abruptly left the school. His class was left without a teacher and there was no immediate successor. This must have caused quite a commotion in the school, especially since he had told nobody except Emil Mol about his plans.

Oehlschlegel decided to travel to Switzerland, Italy, and Venezuela first before making his way back to the United States, where he was planning to gather financial support for a movement of social reform including the introduction of Waldorf education and the formation of a Waldorf College. Extant letters show that he first felt a strong connection to Stuttgart, but later letters document increasing despair and estrangement.

Over time his letters became fewer and fewer, and contact between him, Molt, and the school gradually ceased altogether, until 1921 when he surfaced in Honolulu. In the meantime, the school inspector in Stuttgart had been informed of the fact that "Oehlschlegel had unilaterally gone beyond his leave of absence and left us without any news from him for over a year", for which reason he was no longer regarded as a teacher at the Waldorf School.

Nothing is known about what became of him, which leaves us with a tragic aftertaste concerning this member of the group of pioneers of the first Waldorf School.

Walter Johannes Stein

Walter Johannes Stein

The festive celebration of September 7, 1919 also marked the end of the preparatory course for the new cohort of teachers, and participants who had not been assigned a task by Rudolf Steiner the day before they were preparing to return to their previous occupations.

This was the situation that Walter Johannes Stein, 28 years old at the time, found himself in. Like Caroline von Heydebrand, he had just completed his last doctoral examinations a few weeks before in Vienna. Indeed, he was the first to write a dissertation about Rudolf Steiner. Next to philosophy, Stein had studied mathematics and physics. He had also put a great deal of effort into promoting the movement for social threefolding in Vienna during the spring and summer of 1919. He had pleaded with Rudolf Steiner for permission to take part in the teachers course in Stuttgart, to which he had not at first been invited. After the ceremony on the 7th, Stein was literally plucked from the street in front of the school by E. A. Karl Stockmeyer, who gave him the assignment from Rudolf Steiner to serve as a substitute teacher. Stein must have been overjoyed to be asked, and he was inwardly prepared to give his all to this new task.

Stein spent the first weeks in grade one, substituting for Leonie von Mirbach, the first grade teacher. By the end of November 1919, however, it became clear that Rudolf Treichler, who alternated with E. A. Karl Stockmeyer in teaching grades 7 and 8, had to focus all his efforts on teaching foreign languages. Though a natural scientist by training, Walter Johannes Stein now had to teach German and history. With characteristic zeal, he strove to penetrate the subjects which were foreign territory for him up to then, and he taught them brilliantly.

"In spite of his quiet, modest manner, which made any outer form of disciplinary measures unnecessary, he commanded unquestioning authority because of his spiritual power." (Rudolf Grosse)

In the early years, Rudolf Steiner singled him and Caroline von Heydebrand out for praise for his ability to imbue his lesson material with anthroposophical understanding.

Stein combined teaching with an extensive lecturing schedule; he was also a prolific anthroposophical author. The themes he covered were many: in addition to educational topics in the context of contemporary politics, Waldorf pedagogy, and history, he also lectured on anthroposophy and Rudolf Steiner's work. Stein also set himself the task of protecting Rudolf Steiner against numerous attacks from various quarters. He did it with expertise, courage, and verbal acumen that were unbeatable, even feared.

Working together with a faculty of highly gifted and anthroposophically trained colleagues—Herbert Hahn and Caroline von Heydebrand, to name but two—was a source of great happiness for Stein. His good friends and fellow students from Vienna, Eugen Kolisko and Hermann von Baravalle, soon joined the Stuttgart school, much to his delight.

After a short time, however, Stein went through a deep professional and personal crisis, which was compounded by the many extra activities he had taken on. Instead of really teaching, he tended to lecture, holding high school students captive by propounding anthroposophical theses. This led to estrangement in the high school and discipline problems. Rudolf Steiner was upset and criticized Stein just as unsparingly as he had praised him two years before for his exemplary teaching.

Stein was shocked about himself and questioned his own capacity as a teacher. Two elements sustained him through this crisis: a boundless devotion to Rudolf Steiner's authority and an iron will. This combination helped him to overcome what he had to face and made him a brilliant teacher again.

After the death of Rudolf Steiner—news of which he had to bring to the faculty—Stein went through a very difficult time involving many tensions and conflicts as people struggled with the question of how to continue anthroposophical work and uphold the life of the Anthroposophical Society. Stein felt compelled to take an uncompromising stance, which often led to polarization. In the end, he left Germany in 1932 and moved to England. He did not work as a teacher there, however, but as a journalist, lecturer, and coordinator. Surprisingly, he developed therapeutic capacities and worked as a curative practitioner until his death in London in 1957.

Alexander Strakosch

Alexander Strakosch

In the spring of 1920, it became clear that there was a group of eighth graders that would not be going into the ninth grade, but were looking to transition into practical work. For this group, Rudolf Steiner outlined the following plan, which was to inaugurate a so-called "Fortbildungsschule", a continuation school. "For them, one has to emphasize the practical and artistic side. They need to acquire concepts of life, agriculture, business, industry, trade. They should learn about business letters, accounting, and, as far as the artistic side is concerned, sculpting, music, and literature. I think Mr. Strakosch is the man to make this his task. Life should be seen as a school. One can tell them again and again that life will teach them from this point onward."

At the time, however, Alexander Strakosch held a prestigious position as an engineer working for the Austrian railroads. It was a good thing that he had been able to participate in the teachers' course held in Stuttgart during the summer of 1919. Not only did he have an eminent academic and technical command of his field, but he was also passionate about Greek literature and philosophy, was an excellent violinist, a good horseman, and a virtuoso skater. What is more, he was fluent in four languages. Through his wife, a student of Kandinsky, he was in touch with the visual arts.

He had met anthroposophy in 1908 and felt very connected to it and to Rudolf Steiner. Strakosch knew him very well, not only because he had attended several lecture courses, but also because he had become further acquainted personally, for example by spending a holiday together with Rudolf Steiner and his wife Marie in Istria in 1911.

During the teachers course Strakosch celebrated his 40th birthday, which in a young circle of colleagues made him one of the oldest participants. With his "remarkable face, framed by a black beard", the government-appointed engineer commanded a natural respect among the other course participants. He soon became very much beloved, because he was "lovable and open, almost the way Mediterranean people tend to be" (Herbert Hahn).

In the spring of 1920 Strakosch was asked to give up his position with the Austrian government, move to Stuttgart, and devote himself the Stuttgart Waldorf School. Sadly, it wasn't possible at the time to realize the idea of the "continuation school" because Strakosch had to fill an immediate, pressing need and take over the fifth grade, which was suddenly left without a class teacher. Class teaching seemed like second nature to him; it was as if he had never done anything else. Through him the students were able to absorb a rich stream of pictures of contemporary life, rich in the kind of images for which they were longing. One of his students was Rolf Gutbrod, who later became one of the most important postwar architects in Germany. He cherished very special memories of his class teacher, "who had been responsible for building railroads in the mountains of Austria and told us breathtaking stories as well as accounts of the Italian migrant workers." For Rolf, these stories must have opened up vistas for his future profession. One can say that Strakosch was already imparting education for everyday life, the subject which was to become one of his most important pioneering tasks later on.

Right from the start, Strakosch also assumed responsibility for a branch of a new scientific research institute devoted to biology, physics, chemistry, and textile fibers overseen by the organization responsible for "Der Kommende Tag" [The Coming Day, Inc.]

When new arrangements were made at the Waldorf School during the third school year, five practical subjects were instituted for the ninth grade, of which Strakosch took on spinning, weaving, and technical engineering. In the fourth year of the school, his seventh grade had reached a size of sixty-five students and was split in two. Only during the summer of 1924, after he had passed the students on to eighth grade, was he able to take on the technology teaching in the high school, a task which greatly suited him because of his interests and training.

Strakosch very much wanted the school to be up on the latest developments in society. "His achievements in this respect are unforgettable for all of his students. The feminine half of the student body may not have always been open to the latest technical achievements of our time, but because of his humor and his ability to be present in the moment when answering objections, Strakosch managed to win over even those who were hesitant and held back."

He was a personality who was to play a very important role in the Waldorf School. Above all he was a practical teacher—that is to say, someone who derived his educational qualifications directly from his experiences in life. Rudolf Steiner expected not only that the lessons would be refreshed by people like him, but also that they would enliven the social edifice of the school as a whole.

Because of his Jewish heritage, Strakosch was forced by the Nazis to leave the school in 1934, after which he settled in Switzerland, where he lived till the end of his life in 1958.

Karl Schubert

Karl Schubert

Early in 1920, Emil Molt received a remarkable application letter from Karl Schubert, a linguist, asking "whether I could be employed in the factory which you lead, either to work with my hands or otherwise work spiritually." Schubert was invited to come immediately and give a demonstration lesson in the presence of Rudolf Steiner. Even though the lesson went well, there was an embarrassing moment when Schubert fell over as he was trying to pick up a piece of paper from the floor. Steiner smiled and said to him, "You won't take this as a bad omen, I hope."

Starting in April 1920, Steiner gave him a very special—perhaps the most difficult—pedagogical task in the school, which was to head the so-called extra help class. Soon after the school had started, it became clear that quite a few children of the workers' families had the greatest difficulties fitting in with their grade level. Doubling classes was not an option in the Waldorf school, and neither was dismissing the students, so in the morning they were sent for an hour to be with Schubert in the extra help class, after which they could function better in the context of their grade for the rest of the day.

To begin with, there were nine children from grades 1 to 6. But Schubert could work on this task for only about two months, because he had to take over a fourth grade which had lost its teacher. Then, in September, he took the seventh grade and for the next two years he had them for the majority of their main lessons. During the first years he did a lot of foreign language teaching, especially in the upper grades, as well as teaching history.

Schubeth's wide-ranging knowledge of languages came in handy (after all, he spoke French, English, Russian, and Czech fluently, not to mention Ancient Greek and Latin), as well as his universal erudition and culture. The extra help class he led could only be opened again in the fourth year of the school, 1922. The central indication Steiner gave to Schubert was to "wake the children up in the core of their being", counting on his special heart forces to serve others ("courage to serve"), his morality, and his deep humanity, qualities which made it possible for him to become the first Waldorf remedial teacher, long before Steiner gave the so-called remedial education course in 1924. During this lecture cycle, Steiner remarked, "It truly is a blessing to have Dr. Schubert with us; when children join the extra help class, it doesn't take long before they become extremely fond of Dr. Schubert, for his character and temperament awaken the children's love to such an extent that they don't want to leave anymore."

Karl Schubert, an intensely religious man, was able to combine the anthroposophical path of knowledge with his Catholic roots. Anthroposophy resonated deeply with him, and he was able to place the human being in a larger cosmic connection. His many lectures, in which he gave all-encompassing cosmic pictures, were valued highly. Rudolf Steiner himself once said of him: "Dr. Schubert worked very convincingly on people to bring home the truth of the Waldorf school as a whole".

It was largely due to Schubert that the nativity plays from Oberufer were introduced into the life of the Stuttgart school from 1921 onwards. Schubert, who played the important role of the "Treesinger", described the pedagogical effect on the school community in this way: "Waldorf pedagogy depends on loving devotion, which must be there in the same way the shepherds are moved by searching humility. Likewise, this pedagogy must be enlightened by knowledge of the human being which recognizes our eternal core, in the same way that the kings are impelled by their search for wisdom. The greatest pedagogical power lies in recognition of the essence of the human being".

Schubert's capacity to serve came out especially in two areas. He taught the school's religion lessons and he recorded faculty meetings as their stenographer. In this capacity he left both highly precise records of faculty meetings and many lectures, among them Steiner's remedial education lectures.

In the course of the years, there was a shift in direction of the extra help class, which began to take in truly difficult cases, that is to say children who could not take part in the regular classes at all. Karl Schubert taught the extra help class uninterruptedly for a number of years, a great blessing for the children entrusted into his care as well as for the school as a whole, until he was forced by the Nazi regime to leave the school in 1934 because of his Jewish background. Despite his removal from the school, he managed to go on teaching his extra help class "underground" right through to the end of the war in 1945. It was therefore a bitter experience for him to accept that, when the school reopened shortly after the end of the war, it was no longer possible to accommodate him in the schedule either as a remedial educator or as the teacher of the "extra help" class.

Elisabeth and Paul Baumann
Marriage of the Arts in the Waldorf School

Elisabeth Baumann

Paul Baumann

In addition to eight class teachers, Rudolf Steiner invited four subject teachers to be part of the team that was summoned to Stuttgart to build up the new school. First among these specialist teachers were Paul and Elisabeth Baumann. From day one, they dedicated themselves fully to the task of shaping the arts curriculum.

Paul Baumann, born in 1889, attended the grammar school in Karlsruhe, where he met E.A. Karl Stockmeyer, who would later introduce him to anthroposophy. Baumann worked as a music conductor at several German theaters before World War I, and after completing military service, he landed in Zürich, where he joined the anthroposophical movement for the threefold social organism. There he met Elisabeth Dollfuss, a eurythmist eight years his junior, whom he married on the last day of the preparatory course for Waldorf teachers, just before the festive opening of the Stuttgart school.

Elisabeth, who grew up in an anthroposophical family, spent a number of years in anthroposophical circles in Munich. There she studied eurythmy with Lory Smits and was soon giving courses herself. As a twenty-four-year-old, she would become the youngest member of the faculty of Waldorf teachers.

The pair was like a living picture of the manner in which the arts—in their case music and eurythmy—could be married in Waldorf education. "Everyone was overjoyed, and wished the couple well from the bottom of their hearts" (Emil Molt). From then on, they both devoted themselves with great energy to the task of building up the music and eurythmy curriculum, permeating the school with art. This started right from the moment of the opening celebration, for which Paul played music by J.S. Bach and Elisabeth performed eurythmy. They were the center of all the monthly assemblies and Christmas celebrations.

Paul Baumann composed the majority of the musical contributions himself. Right from the beginning, he also started writing about the pedagogical aims of the school. He lectured about the place of eurythmy and music in the new art of education, for example on October 1920 at the first anthroposophical "Hochschulkurs" [advanced course] in Dornach. His lasting contribution, however, is the body of musical compositions he wrote for the new school, including many songs which arose from a revolutionary, new musical impulse. The songs pointed the way to original creation, springing from entirely sovereign sources.

There were no existing school traditions upon which Baumann could build. He composed songs with courage and verve, basing himself on anthroposophical insights and the impulse of freedom impulse that permeated the new pedagogy and art of education. His compositions "were meant to join in the growing chorus with which we appeal to all human beings, striving to save education from being stifled by restrictions imposed by political parties or the state.... These songs could only arise in independent schools, in consonance with a curriculum which couples practical aims for everyday life with the true demands of education as recognized by Rudolf Steiner's anthroposophy, and the psychological insights resulting from it. These songs could only come into being within a collaborative group of teachers who never ceased to work on themselves in order to throw off tendencies of narrowmindedness or abstract prescriptions imposed by conventional pedagogical theories. When these songs succeed in breathing something of the spirit of the Waldorf school, and if listeners are touched by that breath, the songs will have fulfilled their mission."

Baumann's songs are elevated in style; he sets poems to music by poets such as Christian Morgenstern ("Ich bin die Mutter Sonne") and Johann Wolfgang von Goethe. Moreover, he himself wrote idealistic poems of high caliber. Following indications by Rudolf Steiner, he experimented with the way words and music go together. The melody largely follows the natural flow of the syllables, whereby the harmony in the rhyming syllables creates added musical emphasis the way melisma used to do, adding an extra dimension to what the poem expresses. In the songs he composed for the Waldorf school, Baumann thus created an unmistakable style of his own, which following generations picked up and developed further. He also composed sacred music for the services which were held in connection with the new free religion lessons developed in the first Waldorf School.

Baumann's wife Elisabeth was not only the first eurythmist to develop pedagogical eurythmy alongside artistic eurythmy. She also observed that many children had health problems after the war or needed help to overcome hindrances in their development. This prompted her to ask Rudolf Steiner to give indications for hygienic and therapeutic applications of eurythmy, which in turn led to the therapeutic eurythmy course given in Dornach in 1921. It is thanks to her initiative that we now have therapeutic eurythmy.

Paul and Elisabeth Baumann worked at the Waldorf school in Stuttgart until 1937, right up to a few months before it had to close its doors. At that point, they retired from teaching and spent the rest of their lives in France and Switzerland.

Elisabeth von Grunelius

Elisabeth von Grunelius

A large number of outstanding teachers, women and men, put their stamp on the first years of the Waldorf School. Even though the scope of this booklet allows us to honor only a few of them, others should be mentioned at least by name. Among them are pastor Johannes Geyer, who worked as a class teacher. Then there was Rudolf Treichler, one of the first language teachers, who went on to become a class teacher. Two highly gifted pedagogues merit special mentioning, Robert Killian and Christoph Boy, both of whom came with considerable experience from their teaching in educational reform schools, the country school Haubinda and the Odenwald School. We should also mention the painter and craft teacher Max Wolffhügel, Hedwig Hauck, the handwork teacher, the mathematician Hermann von Baravalle, and Fritz Graf von Bothmer, who developed what are now called "Bothmer gymnastics" for the school.

To close this series of mini-portraits, we should paint a small picture of a woman who was there all the time, albeit somewhat in the background at first. But she was to play a highly important part later on. This was Elisabeth von Grunelius.

The original intention was to have a kindergarten up and running on the school grounds by Easter of 1920. It was to serve a large group of children who would then enter first grade after the summer holidays. The attempt to carve out space seems to have yielded no results, because after a brief provisional arrangement, the effort was broken off in May 1920.

Rudolf Steiner had invited Elisabeth von Grunelius, whom he had known since 1914, to be the first kindergarten teacher. She was a delicate young lady who had come to Dornach to work on the carving of the capitals of the first Goetheanum when she was 19 years old. Born in Alsace, she had completed the Comenius kindergarten seminar in Bonn in 1914, and wanted to go on from there to study psychology. After a year and a half in Dornach, she took a leave of absence and went to Berlin in order to do a practicum for kindergarten, nursery, and social work in order to obtain her diploma in the Pestalozzi-Fröbel-Seminar, which would qualify her to train students.

After the war, she returned to Alsace, which by then had become French territory. When Rudolf Steiner asked her to join the faculty of the first Waldorf school, she came, but worked only as a substitute teacher for some time. Rudolf Steiner frequently mentions how difficult it was to fit a kindergarten into the existing configuration of the school grounds. As late as April 1923, Steiner is recorded as saying in one of the faculty meetings that "we can't even think of a kindergarten at the present time".

During the second year of the school's existence, Elizabeth assisted Leonie von Mirbach by taking over the second half of main lesson. In the third school year, that class of 52 children was split into two, and she took one half (3b). After one year of that, she left to study eurythmy and painting in Dornach.

It was only in 1924 that the school managed to carve out a place to build the kindergarten, tucked in a far corner of the playground. This was largely due to the energetic efforts of Herbert Hahn, and the kindergarten was ready for occupancy in 1926. From then on, Elisabeth von Grunelius built up the kindergarten. Since Steiner had died in 1925, she didn't have his direct indications during the initial build-up phase, so it was she who outlined the original foundations of the kindergarten work in the Waldorf school. Later she went on to found the international Waldorf kindergarten movement. She died in 1989, at age 94, the last member of the original faculty at the Stuttgart school.

Made in the USA
Lexington, KY
11 December 2019